BONSAI MAKING HANDBOOK

ALL YOU NEED TO KNOW ABOUT BONSAI AND IT'S MAKING

JAMIE WALLACE

Table of Contents

CHAPTER ONE

BONSAI

To Begin With, What Is Bonsai?

Having a basic familiarity with bonsai is helpful before we dive in.

Bonsai is a Japanese loanword that refers to the practice of growing miniature trees through careful pruning and training.

The resulting plants are also often referred to as by this word in its noun form.

The term "bonsai" is a portmanteau of the Chinese words bon (container) and sai (tree). Tree in a small pot is the sense conveyed by the merged terms.

This is not the same as selectively breeding dwarf plants; rather, it involves keeping normal-sized plants from reaching their full potential by limiting their root growth and cutting back on their foliage. This is where landscaping and creative expression meet.

Although popularized by the Japanese, this technique has its roots in China, where it was known as pun-sai or pen-jing more than two millennia ago.

After Buddhist monks brought bonsai to Japan from China, the Japanese began to make it their own some 1,300 years later.

The practice of bonsai was and is used by Buddhist monks as a means of meditation and achieving a meditative state of flow.

While it’s meant to be a feast for the eyes and is treated as a visual art form, much as sculptures or paintings are, it’s also a discipline that requires patience and skill on the part of the practitioner, artist, or hobbyist.

After WWII, American servicemen began bringing artifacts back from their travels around the world, including bonsai.

Inevitably, that art has been commercialized to the point where you can buy plastic representations today that give you the look without all the work. I get the desire to save time, but it seems to me that that would be counterproductive.

Bonsai can be done by anyone without the need for expensive equipment or a large financial investment. If you want to start your own, all you need is a cutting from a tree in your yard and a yogurt container to grow it in. Your plant could even be grown from seed.

However, you can also buy trees that have already been started, as well as a wide variety of attractive pots in which to grow your plant. There are also a range of tools that you can purchase to make the job easier, though many people prefer to stick to the basics.

As with any art, there are various price points for the aficionado, ranging from downright cheap to priceless. There are bonsai trees that have been grown for centuries, given as gifts, and never put up for sale. They have no quantifiable monetary worth whatsoever.

A Japanese white pine (Pinus parviflora) estimated to be several hundred years old sold at auction for over $1 million at the 2011 Asia-Pacific Bonsai and Suiseki Convention & Exhibition in Takamatsu, Kagawa, Japan.

Pre-started young trees are available for less than $20, making them affordable for the rest of us. You can find untrained seedlings of plants that make good bonsai for much less money.

It’s easy to become all wrapped up in the art of bonsai, but don’t feel overwhelmed. Whatever level of complexity you desire is entirely up to you.

CHAPTER TWO

Making Bonsai: The Art and Craft

The point of this activity is to recreate a miniature version of nature indoors. In its natural habitat, the tree should serve as inspiration for the composition... only in miniature.

Some of them are standing completely upright, while others appear to have been frozen in a gust of wind. One tree may be shown in some cases, while multiple trees may be shown in others.

Indoor bonsai are rare, but some can be grown from seed.

The chosen plant is placed in a small pot, usually one that is low and wide, though you can use tall and deep pots as well.

The tree is then routinely pruned and the roots are trimmed periodically to keep the plant constrained. When a plant is young, it may also be trained to grow into a specific shape using wire, though not every artist does this step.

Farmers model their techniques after the plant's wild growth pattern. A ginkgo tree usually won’t be trained into a weeping shape, and a weeping cherry won’t be forced to grow upright.

Some might say it's cruel to keep trees in pots. Don't worry though. In other words, the tree is unharmed.

Pruning plants' leaves and branches is an ancient practice. It is a time-honored practice in gardening to limit the size of a plant by cutting back on its roots. And people have been using pots to cultivate plants ever since they were first created.

It's not an exaggeration to say that bonsai plants receive more TLC than many wild trees because of the special attention they receive.

Similarly, you may be wondering how long it will take to make a truly stunning example.

Depending on the species (hello, rosemary!) and the age of the plant you start with, it can take as little as a few years or as long as several decades.

CHAPTER THREE

Styles

There are roughly 15 different ways that plants can be trained to grow. There are five distinct types, including the upright, slanted, cascading, and semi-cascading styles.

Try not to force yours into any of the boxes we've drawn here. If your tree is expressing a desire to undergo a transformation, you should honor that desire.

Bonsai is an art form with no universally accepted rules. It's all up to you and what you can see and imagine.

Still, knowing the various approaches can serve as a useful springboard. Okay, let's check this out.

Bunjingi (Literati)

As an example of the bunjingi aesthetic, think of a tree in a forest full of other trees.

To compete with other plants, it must grow tall, and the surrounding tree canopy will prevent it from developing lower branches.

In most cases, the trunk is curved in a way that suggests the tree twisted its way upward in search of better lighting.

Where did that strange name come from? Some may even draw parallels between these and the slender, abstract, winding trees found in famous Chinese literati paintings.

Chokkan (Formal Upright)

It's a common aesthetic choice in bonsai, and it's also found frequently in nature.

The plant is tall and erect, with a thin, slender trunk and many branches.

Fukinagashi (Windswept)

It appears that the fukinagashi tree has been growing in a very windy area.

There will be a noticeable lean to it, and the branches will all grow in the same direction, though they can emerge from the trunk at any angle.

Han-Kengai (Semi-Cascading)

This style, called semi-cascading, is meant to evoke the swaying of cliffside trees buffeted by high winds.

Semi-cascades, in contrast to cascades, grow laterally and downward but never beyond the container's rim.

Hokidachi (Broom)

The plant's form, known as broom style, will be that of a broom: a single trunk from which numerous fine branches radiate outward.

The shape of the ball is achieved by shaping the branches.

Ikadabuki (Raft)

Have you ever seen a fallen tree in the forest from which new, upright trees sprouted? That's the kind of aesthetic this evokes.

A single trunk, growing perpendicular to the pot's surface, will branch off into several additional trunks. Over time, the lower trunk usually rots away, leaving the new trees to grow with their roots at a higher level.

One drawback to this flashy method of cultivation is that it isn't appropriate for every plant species. The most successful trees include juniper, quince, spruce, ficus, beech, olive, and pine.

Ishizuki (Growing-in-Rock)

Similarities can be drawn between this and the seki-joju style, which will be discussed in more detail down the page. A tree grows within a rock, with its roots settling into the crevices rather than on top of the rock, as in the case of the latter.

If you choose this style, you'll need to be very conscientious about keeping it well-watered and fertilized.

Kabudachi (Multi-Trunk)

More than two trunks emerge from the main trunk and share a single root system in this design.

Because they come from the same tree, the trunks are not distinct.

Kengai (Cascading)

This dramatic cascade form gives the impression that the plant is perched precariously on the edge of a cliff and is being regularly squished by falling snow or rocky outcrops. The tree's trunk needs some upward growth before it can curve downward.

You'll want to use a tall container for this look, and you'll have to train your plant to grow downward at regular intervals because it will resist your efforts. If done properly, however, it can be stunning in its elegance.

Moyogi (Informal Upright)

Moyogi trees have trunks that resemble the letter "S" and narrow toward the top. Each arc gives rise to an individual branch.

This is a common style for evergreens like juniper. The apex should be located in line with the base of the trunk, but the trunk can weave and curve all it wants in the middle.

Seki-Joju (Growing-on-Rock)

Picture a rocky mountain face and the tough trees that make their home by finding nutrition in the cracks and holes between the rocks. That's what this style seeks to recreate.

The tree is grown on a rock with the roots extending over the rock and into the soil below.

Shakan (Slanting)

This style recreates a tree that is buffeted by a constant, steady, light wind. It can also resemble a tree that is growing in the shade of a large building or another tree.

The tree's trunk will bend in one direction, either to follow the sun's rays or to avoid the wind. To prevent the tree from looking lopsided, the lowest branch should develop in the opposite direction of the lean.

A tree in this style is gently leaning back from the ground at an angle of 60 degrees to 80 degrees, whereas fukinagashi trees appear to be in the process of being blown over by strong winds.

Sharimiki (Driftwood)

Sharimiki is less a shape than it is a technique whereby strips of bark are removed to give the impression that the tree is damaged, partially dead, or old. Lime sulfur will be used to bleach these bare components.

CHAPTER FOUR

The Three Easy Steps to Planting Your Own Bonsai Tree (And Keep It Alive Afterwards)

Bonsai (Japanese for "tree in a tray or pot") is a form of living sculpture that always looks beautiful and impressive. But they're just regular trees that somebody has pruned down to dwarf size on purpose, then shaped into a variety of forms or even miniature landscapes. More than two thousand years ago, bonsai found its first home in China, where it flourished for a while before finding greater success in Japan. The miniature scale of this art form uniquely expresses Zen concepts of nature, elements, and change. Given the proper care and attention, many valuable specimens can live for hundreds of years and are thus passed down from generation to generation.

Your own bonsai can be grown from seed or cuttings you collect from your garden or from a nearby nursery. Perhaps you have a maple tree that produces a flood of tiny helicopters that you can use to start your own bonsai. Kits are available for purchase that include seeds ideal for bonsai. Bonsai can be made from any kind of tree or shrub, evergreen or deciduous; even annual bloomers like azaleas, crabapples, or wisteria work well.

Techniques for Growing a Bonsai

Because bonsai are usually kept in shallow pots while being trained, they require daily watering during the warmer months. Hardy bonsai can remain outdoors in the winter as long as they are shielded from drying wind and direct sunlight, while more delicate specimens should be brought indoors or to a greenhouse.

Prep Root Ball

Take the plant out of its pot and prune off the bottom two-thirds of the root mass. Rake the top layer of soil away to reveal the plant's underground structure. Apply liquid from a spray bottle to the roots of the plant.

Put root ball in pot

Cut away any limbs that aren't contributing to the overall look you're going for, as well as any that are obviously dead. If there are any dead roots or large roots that will get in the way of potting, you should get rid of them. Plant it, then fill in the soil around its roots. Water thoroughly, then cover the soil with gravel or moss.

Tree Shaping

To begin, you must identify the branches that need pruning and shaping. Wrap wire tightly enough to achieve the desired shape but not so tightly that growth is stunted (this will help guide the branch to grow in the direction and shape you want). Cut the wire back once the branch has matured enough to maintain its new form.

What to Do After You've Planted Your Bonsai

You can't just water and forget about your bonsai like you would any other houseplant after you've planted it. If you follow these guidelines, you can keep it in great condition forever.

Watering

Phylum Type A This trick may not go over well with mom and dad, but it's the most reliable method of giving your bonsai the proper amount of water. To avoid over-watering, you should never do so regularly. Although you may have a set schedule for watering your other houseplants, such as every Saturday, your bonsai trees require more nuanced care. Irrigate instead when the soil is almost dry to the touch.

Fertilizing

Most bonsai trees, as a general rule, should be fertilized all through the growing season (early spring to mid-fall). However, fertilization requirements can shift depending on the species of tree you're tending to. Use either a granular or liquid fertilizer; there are even fertilizers designed specifically for bonsai trees. For optimum results, use as directed on the label.

Soil

Mixtures of Akadama (hard-baked clay), pumice, lava rock, and soil are commonly used as bonsai soil. You'll have to try different permutations until you find one that suits you. It's important for bonsai soil to be able to hold water without soaking the roots.

Repotting

Repotting your bonsai tree every two years is recommended for young trees, while older trees can stay in the same pot for up to five years. If you look at the bottom of the container and see the roots growing in a circle, it's time to repot. If your tree needs to be repotted, now is the time to do it, as it will be dormant and easier to work with. The soil mixture shouldn't be drastically different from the one the tree was previously acclimated to, so keep that in mind as you move the tree to a larger pot.

THE END

www.ingramcontent.com/pod-product-compliance
Lightning Source LLC
LaVergne TN
LVHW010509160826
845677LV00012B/2747

* 9 7 9 8 8 4 7 0 7 4 8 3 4 *